WONDERFUL YOU

Library of Congress Cataloging-in-Publication Data

Burstein, John.
The body / by Slim Goodbody ; illustrated by Terry Boles.
        p.   cm. — (Wonderful you)
Summary: Presents simple verses, experiments, fun facts, and health advice about different body parts and functions.
ISBN 0-925190-85-3
1. Human anatomy—Juvenile literature. [1. Human anatomy. 2. Human physiology. 3. Body, Human.] I. Boles, Terry, ill. II. Title. III. Series: Wonderful you (Minneapolis, Minn.)
QM27.B87   1996
612—dc20

96-13183
CIP
AC

Cover design by Barry Littmann.

First Printing: October 1996
Printed in the United States of America

00 99 98 97 96   7 6 5 4 3 2 1

Published by Fairview Press, 2450 Riverside Avenue South, Minneapolis, MN 55454.

For a current catalog of Fairview Press titles, please call this Toll-Free number: 1-800-544-8207

Publisher's Note: Fairview Press publishes books and other materials related to the subjects of family and social issues. Its publications, including *The Body,* do not necessarily reflect the philosophy of Fairview Hospital and Healthcare Services or their treatment programs.

The paper used in this publication meets the minimum requirements of American National Standard for Information Sciences—Permanence of Paper for Printed Library Materials, ANSI Z329.48-1984.

THE BODY

Slim Goodbody

illustrated by Terry Boles

Fairview Press
Minneapolis

The Body Symphony

Your body is incredible—
It's busy every minute.
Amazing things are happening
To keep you living in it.

Your mind is thinking,
Eyes are blinking,
Your hair and nails are growing.
Your lungs are breathing,
Heart is beating,
And your blood is flowing.

Billions of cells are working together,
All in harmony.
You're a song of life created by
The body symphony.

Skin

First of all, let's begin with skin,
Which wraps you up, and keeps you in.
From the top of your head
To the soles of your feet,
It helps keep out cold
And helps hold in heat.
It's a colorful covering germs can't get through,
Designed to protect the inside of you.
And because we have skin,
We are able to touch
And feel all the things
In the world around us.

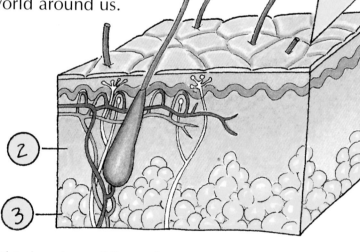

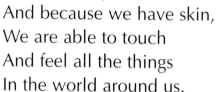

Skin has three different layers:

1 The outer layer is always flaking off and being replaced with skin from below.

2 The middle layer contains blood vessels, nerve endings, and hair roots.

3 The inner layer is mainly fat.

Experiment

To understand how your skin keeps you cool when you're hot

Lick your index finger up to the first joint. When it is nice and wet, wave it in the air to dry it off. Which part of your finger gets the coolest?

Explanation: When your body gets over-heated, you start to sweat through your skin. As the sweat dries, it gives off heat into the air and you cool off.

Amazing Fact!

✔ The skin's top layer contains one color pigment. It is called *melanin.* Everyone has different amounts of this pigment and so everybody's skin color is different. But no matter what the color, everybody's skin works exactly the same way.

Experiment

To appreciate your skin's sense of touch

Find an apple, an orange, and a piece of sandpaper. Use your fingertips to feel each one. Notice how each one feels different. Now put on a pair of gloves (leather would be best) and feel all three again. What happened to your ability to feel the differences? What does this tell you about your sense of touch?

Explanation: You have special *touch receptors* in your fingertips that send messages to your brain about what you touch. When you wear gloves, these receptors can't get any information from the objects you touch. You also have other receptors that send special reports to your brain about temperature, pain, and pressure.

Amazing Facts!

✔ The skin you are wearing today isn't the same skin that covered you yesterday! That's because the outer layer of your skin is always flaking off and being replaced by new skin from layers below. And if skin gets cut, it has the amazing ability to grow back together!

✔ Just one square inch of skin (on the back of your hand) has almost 20,000 touch receptors sending messages to your brain.

Amazing Facts!

✔ Skin has different thicknesses depending on where it is on your body and what it's used for. The skin on your eyelids is much, much thinner than the skin on the soles of your feet.

✔ Your skin is waterproof! Next time you wash your hands, or take a bath or shower, be glad that water can't get inside!

Healthy Advice

✔ Dirt and germs can get caught in the folds and wrinkles and on the surface of your skin. Washing removes them. To keep your body nice and clean:

1 Wash your hands with lots of soap and water before eating and after going to the bathroom.

2 Shower or take a bath as often as necessary— at least once every other day.

✔ When you get cut or scraped, be sure to clean the area very well to wash away dirt and germs. Your mom or dad may want to help.

✔ When the sun is strong and you're outside, protect your skin from any harmful rays by using a good sunblock lotion and wearing a hat.

Hair

If your head was a bed,
Then your hair would be the spread—
A protective covering
Of black, brown, blond, or red.

Hair grows out of tiny holes called *follicles.* The shape of these holes
determines the kind of hair a person has.

2 Wavy hair grows
from oval follicles.

3 Straight hair
grows from
round follicles.

1 Curly hair grows
from flat follicles.

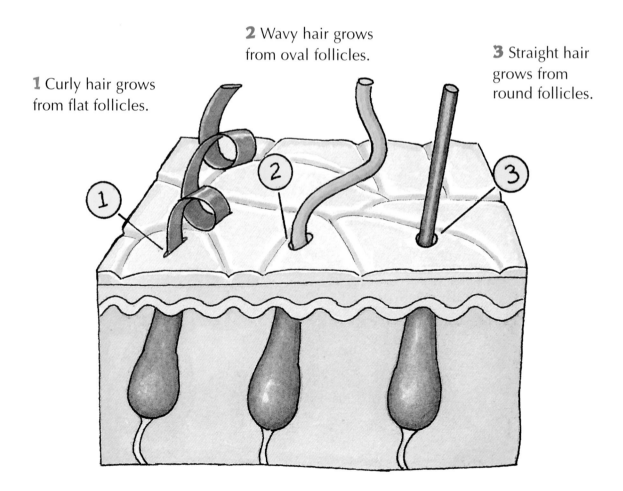

Experiment To see how hair stretches

With the help of an adult, carefully cut a piece of hair about three inches long from your head or that of friend or family member. Tape a penny to one end, and tape the other end to the inside lid of a jar. Screw the lid on carefully and see how low the penny hangs. With a marker, mark the level on the side of the jar. Wait overnight and mark the level again. What happened?

Explanation: Hair is naturally stretchy. The weight of the penny will stretch it, but not break it.

Healthy Advice

✔ Shampoo your hair several times a week to remove dirt and sweat that gets built up and trapped. Brushing and combing also help bring out your hair's natural shine.

Experiment

To see how hair gives us early warning

Ask a friend or parent to close their eyes. Very carefully, with the point of a pencil, move some arm hairs. Be sure not to touch the skin. Can they feel it?

Explanation: Every hair on your body is connected to a nerve. So even though the pencil didn't touch the skin, it affected the body's sense of touch.

Amazing Facts!

✔ The part of your hair that grows out is no longer living—that's why it doesn't hurt when you get a haircut.

✔ We lose about 80 hairs a day.

✔ Hair is as strong as aluminum. A single hair can hold up to three ounces. If you made a rope out of strands of hair, it could lift a 2,000-pound automobile.

✔ People have an average of 100,000 hairs on their heads.

Brain

Your brain is in charge of all of you—
It controls everything that you say and do.
Your thinking and your feeling,
Your stretching and your kneeling,
Your jawbone when you're talking,
Your feet when you're walking,
Your reading and your writing,
And even your nail biting!
Yes, leading and uniting
Is your brain—
Now that's exciting!

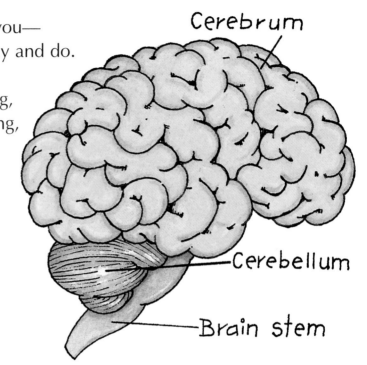

The brain has three different parts. Each does a different job, but all the parts work together:

Making a decision,
Or doing long division?
You use your *cerebrum.* This is where you store information and memories and where you do your thinking. It's also what starts your muscles moving.

Riding a bike,
Or taking a hike?
You use your *cerebellum.* It helps you keep your balance and controls more than 200 sets of muscles.

Breathing, blood flow,
And the speed at which your heart will go.
For these, you use your *brain stem.* It keeps certain parts of your body running smoothly night and day without your having to think about them.

Experiment

To help you understand how the three parts of your brain work together

Stretch out your arm in front of you, then make a circle in the air with your index finger. Finally, touch the tip of your finger to your nose.

Explanation: You used your big cerebrum to read about and understand this experiment. The cerebrum also ordered your muscles to move. Then the smaller cerebellum made sure all the muscles worked together to carry out the order. The brain stem has been controlling your breathing and heartbeat the whole time you've been concentrating on this experiment.

Amazing Fact!

✔ Inside your skull, your brain floats in a special fluid that cushions it from injuries.

Amazing Facts!

✔ Only two creatures in the whole world have larger brains than people—a full-grown elephant and an adult male whale. And that's only because these animals are so much larger than we are.

✔ The right side of your brain controls movement on the left side of your body. The left side of your brain controls movement on the right side!

✔ Some scientists estimate that we use only 10 to 15% of our brain's abilities.

Healthy Advice

✔ Exercise your brain by experiencing, experimenting, reading, thinking, dreaming, and imagining. Your brain will work better and better the more you use it.

✔ When you go bike riding, roller blading, or skate boarding, be sure to wear a safety helmet to protect your head and brain if you should fall.

Nervous System

Through the spinal cord and nerves,
Which branch out everywhere,
Your nervous system's well equipped
To keep your brain aware
Of every touch, taste, and sound,
And all the sights and smells around.

And once this data's been reported
To your brain, it's quickly sorted.
Then, if any action's needed,
Through your nerves an order's speeded,
Telling muscles what to do,
Movements they must make for you.

Your nervous system is designed
For fast communication,
Sending and receiving streams
Of vital information.

The nervous system has three parts:

1 The brain

2 The spinal cord running through
the backbone

3 The countless nerves that branch out
to all parts of the body

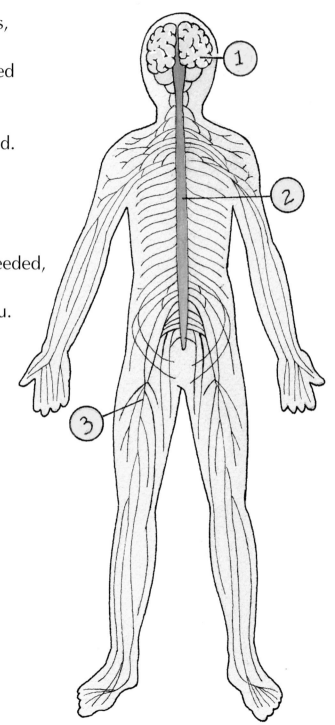

There are two different kinds of nerves:

1 *Sensory nerves* carry messages from your senses to your brain.

2 *Motor nerves* carry messages from your brain to your muscles.

Amazing Facts

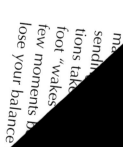

✔ Your nerves can send messages from your brain to your t
feet per second. Four hundred feet is longer than a football
travel in one second!

✔ When you accidentally hit your elbow and it sends a q
your "funny bone." Actually, you have banged a nerve th
down the arm.

ma
send
tions tak
foot "wakes
few moments
lose your balance

Experiment

To see how fast your nerves can send a message

Time how long it takes to get a message from your brain to your toe. Have a friend or parent look at a stopwatch and say "go." Move your toe as soon as you can. How much time went by?

Explanation: Since nerves can send messages at incredible speeds, it only takes a fraction of a second for a message to reach from your brain to your toe. Think about a time when you stepped on something painful, maybe a broken shell at the beach. Sensory nerves shot messages to your brain, and motor nerves flashed orders back. From your foot to your brain and back to your foot—all in an instant!

Healthy Advice

✔ Sometimes when you sit too long in one position, your foot "falls asleep." That's because the ~~m~~ain nerve in your leg gets squeezed and stops ~~sendin~~g messages to your brain. Changing posi-~~tion take~~s the pressure off the nerve, and your ~~foot "wakes up~~" with a tingling feeling. But wait a ~~minute b~~efore you walk on it, or you might ~~stumble a~~nd fall.

The Senses

Letting you know what's going on,
Bringing you pleasure and pain,
Five sensational senses are
Reporting it all to the brain.

What you taste and what you smell,
And everything you touch as well,
What you see and what you hear—
Our world's revealed, sharp and clear.

1 Your eyes are like two cameras taking moving pictures of everything in front of you.

2 Your ears are like radio antennas tuned into the sounds around you.

3 Your nose acts like a special air filter that catches the different odors in the air.

4 Your tongue contains taste buds for gathering up tastes and flavors.

5 Your skin contains special nerve endings called *touch receptors* that allow you to feel what's around you.

Each of your senses works differently, but they all share the same goal—to provide your brain with enough information to avoid danger, and to experience all the wonderful things life has to offer.

Experiment

To fool your sense of taste

Cut up some apples and some pears. Have a friend close his or her eyes. Put the apple in your friend's mouth while you hold the pear under his or her nose. What fruit does your friend think is being eaten?

Explanation: Your senses of taste and smell work together. Often you smell foods when you think you are tasting them. When you're sick and your nose is stuffed up, you can hardly taste anything at all.

Amazing Fact!

✔ There are about 9,000 taste buds inside the bumps on your tongue.

Experiment

To realize how much we depend upon our sense of sight

With a friend's or parent's help, put on a blindfold and walk around your home for a few minutes. Does it feel comfortable or strange?

Explanation: As babies, our sense of touch is the most important. As we grow, we depend more and more upon our sense of sight. When we can't use our eyes, it can make even familiar places seem very scary or strange.

Healthy Advice

✔ You depend a lot upon your sense of sight, so be sure to protect it. If you ever notice any problem, for example, blurry vision, tell a parent or adult right away so it can be checked by a doctor.

Amazing Facts!

✔ Your senses of sight, hearing, and smell are called distance senses, because they bring in information from things at a distance. Taste and touch can only reveal information about things that you actually come in direct contact with.

✔ The loudest sounds we hear are millions of times louder than the softest sounds we can hear.

✔ Your five main senses are not the only ones you have. You have deeper senses to let your know when to eat and drink. You have a sense of balance, of time, of weight, and of distance as well.

Healthy Advice

✔ Your senses do more than help you enjoy and appreciate the world—they also help keep your body safe. When crossing the street, be sure to use your eyes AND ears. You could see cars in one direction and hear a bicycle coming from the other direction.

✔ If you listen to music with earphones, be sure to keep the volume at a reasonable level. If music is too loud, it can damage your hearing.

Heart

Lub-dub, lub-dub,
Inside your chest,
Lub-dub, lub-dub,
No time for rest.
Lub-dub, lub-dub,
Your mighty heart
Is pumping blood
To every part.

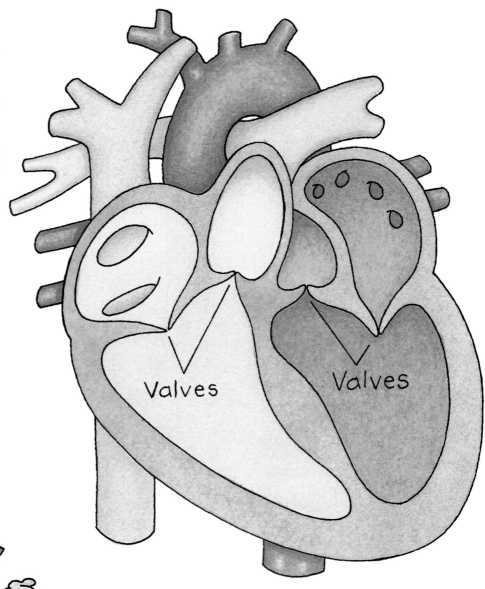

Your heart is a muscle with four rooms, or *chambers*. Valves between the chambers open and close to let blood flow through, making the "lub-dub" sound you hear.

Experiment

To better understand how your heart works

Find an old tennis ball. Cut a little hole in it and fill the ball with water. What happens when you squeeze it? What happens when you relax your grip?

Explanation: Every time your heart beats, it acts something like the tennis ball. The heart muscle squeezes blood out and on its way. Then, between beats, it goes back to its original shape. It refills with blood, then repeats the whole process.

Healthy Advice

✔ Give your heart the exercise it needs to stay strong and healthy. Activities such as running, brisk walking, jump roping, or bike riding are great. Doing these three or four times a week, and staying active for at least fifteen minutes each time, gives you a healthy heart workout sometimes called *aerobic exercise.*

Experiment

To listen to a heart at work

Make your own stethoscope by rolling up a sheet of paper or using the cardboard tube from inside a roll of paper towels. Color your stethoscope your favorite color. Put one end of the stethoscope to a friend's chest and the other end to your ear. Can you hear your friend's heartbeat? (Tip: Move the stethoscope around until the beating comes in loud and clear.)

Explanation: A stethoscope helps collect the "lub-dub" sound so you can hear more clearly.

Amazing Facts!

✔ Your heart is about the same size as your fist and grows at about the same rate.

✔ A baby's heart beats about 135 times per minute. That's faster than a grown-up's heart, which beats about 75 times a minute.

✔ Your heart will beat more than one million times in the next two weeks.

Circulation

Your body's system of circulation
Is an incredible method of transportation,
A river of life that flows under your skin,
Round and around in one direction,
Providing food and air and waste collection
To every single part that lies within.

Blood flows through
Two different lanes,
Out through your arteries
And back through the veins.
From your heart to your lungs
To get some air,
Then back to your heart
To be pumped everywhere.

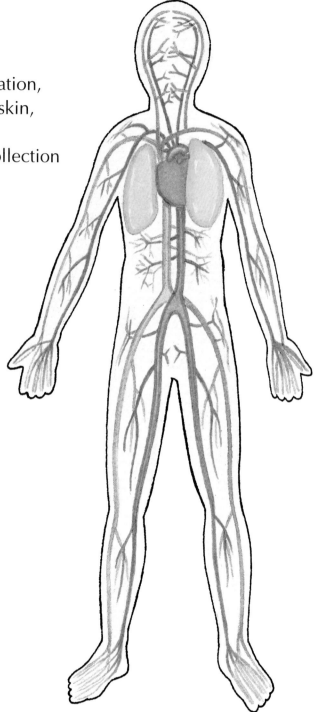

Experiment

To feel the blood rushing through your body

Touch the first two fingers of one hand to (1) The wrist of your other hand right below the thumb (palms up), (2) Your temple, (3) The side of your neck right below your jaw. What do you feel?

Explanation: At these three places, blood runs close to the surface of your skin, and you can feel the pulse.

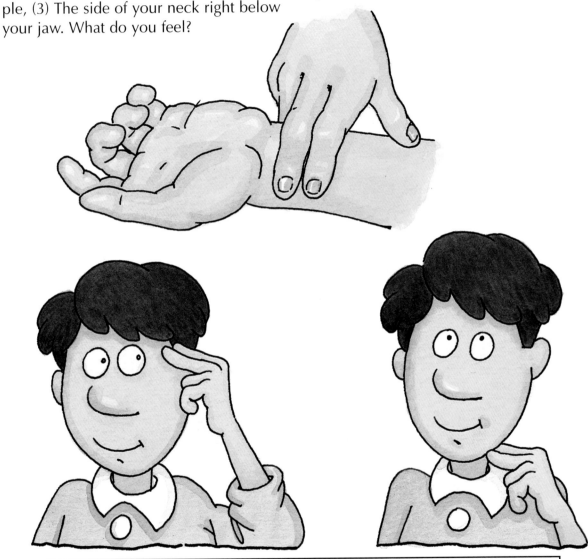

Amazing Fact!

✔ Blood makes the round-trip body journey about 1,000 times a day!

Amazing Facts!

✔ Blood flowing through your body changes colors! When it picks up oxygen in your lungs, it turns bright red. When it drops that oxygen off to your cells, it turns purplish blue.

✔ Your body has between 60,000 and 100,000 MILES of blood vessels. That's the distance you would travel if you went four times around the world.

Healthy Advice

✔ Protect yourself from injuries that might cause bleeding. Don't handle knives or sharp objects without an adult or parent around, and be very careful when you do.

Lungs

You have a pink and lovely pair
Of lungs designed to breathe the air
In and out, that's how air flows
In and out, through mouth or nose

Muscles help you breathe. Your *diaphragm,* the muscle under your lungs, moves down, and other muscles move your ribs up and outward. Your chest gets bigger and air flows in to fill the space. When these muscles relax, the space in your chest gets smaller, and the air is forced out.

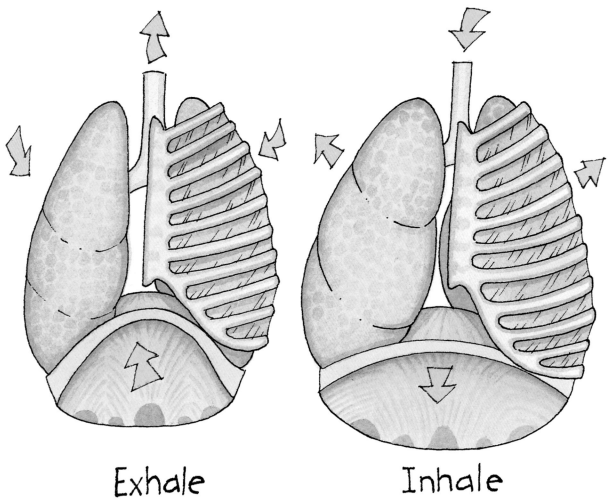

Exhale   Inhale

Experiment

To understand how activity affects breathing

Most people breathe in and out about 17 times a minute when they are relaxed. Check if this is true for you by using a watch or clock with a second hand. Now run in place for a minute and time your breathing again. Do you breathe any faster?

Explanation: Oxygen from the air you breathe is changed by your body into energy. When you exercise, you need more energy. Breathing faster brings your body more oxygen to give you more energy.

Healthy Advice

✔ In order to keep your lungs healthy, don't smoke. If you're around someone who does smoke, try to move away. Otherwise you'll breathe their smoke into your lungs.

Healthy Advice

✔ Breathe in through your nose most of the time. Your nose is a special air tunnel that cleans, warms, and moistens the air before it reaches your lungs.

✔ You can give your lungs the room they need to work well by using good posture.

Amazing Facts!

✔ Your *diaphragm,* the muscle under your lungs, is the second hardest working muscle in your body. Just like your heart muscle, your diaphragm works day and night without ever stopping.

✔ We take about ten million breaths a year!

✔ Babies breathe faster than adults.

Bones

Without your bones, you couldn't stand up.
You wouldn't have much shape at all—
Like a lump of clay, or a jellyfish,
Or a punctured rubber ball.
Yes, to give you shape
And support your weight,
Bones are absolutely great.
Long bones, short bones,
Big bones, small—
You have 206 in all!

All the bones in your body are called
your *skeleton.*

Ribs are like a vest
You wear around your chest
To protect your lungs and heart.
Your cranium surrounds your brain-ium.
Bones guard your softer parts.

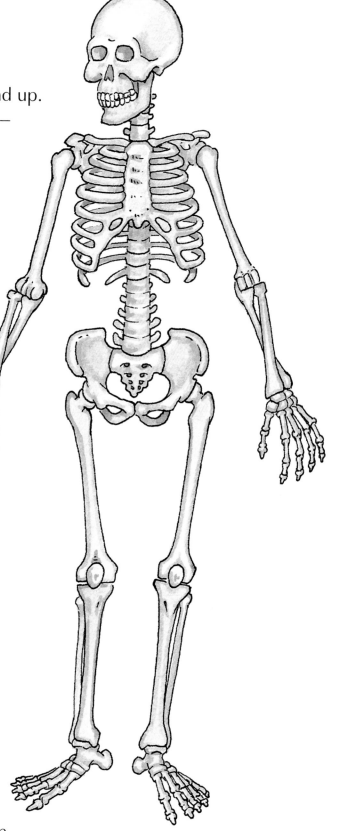

Bones aren't solid. If they were, they'd be too heavy for you to move around. Instead, bones have a hard outer layer over a spongy inside called *marrow*.

Amazing Facts!

✔ Your bones are a blood factory. The marrow inside them manufactures millions and millions of blood cells every day.

✔ Babies have more than 300 bones when they're born. As a child grows older, many of these grow together and form single bones. An adult has 206 bones.

✔ More than half of all the bones in your body are in your wrists, hands, ankles, and feet.

✔ The largest bone in your body is your thighbone. The smallest is the tiny stirrup bone in your inner ear.

Experiment

To see if your height changes during the day

When you first wake up, stand straight by a wall and ask a family member to carefully measure and mark your height. Measure it again at the end of the day. What happened?

Explanation: Your spine is actually made up of many separate bones, all lined up in a row. Soft disks between these bones act as cushions. When you sleep, the disks are plumped with fluid. When you stand during the day, these disks flatten out a bit—and you seem to shrink.

Healthy Advice

✔ Because so many of your bones are in your feet, wearing comfortable and well-fitting shoes is important. Stand up when your feet are measured, because feet spread out when you stand on them. If one foot is longer, buy the shoes that fit the longer foot.

✔ You need to eat food with lots of vitamins and minerals to help your bones grow bigger and stronger. You'll get many of these nutrients from dairy products, fruits, and vegetables.

Joints

Bones come together at different points.
Those different points are known as joints.
At joints bones meet up end to end.
Now, point to a joint that you twist or bend.

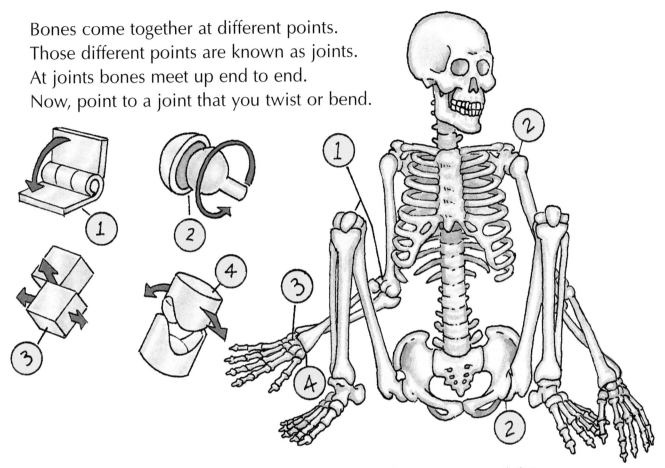

Your joints help give your body all kinds of movement possibilities:

1 *Hinge joints* at your elbows and knees move back and forth
like a door on a hinge and allow you to bend.

2 *Ball and socket joints* at your hips and shoulders let you
twist and turn in many directions.

3 *Sliding joints* at your wrists let the many bones slip and slide
over each other so you can move easily.

4 *Saddle joints* at your thumb let you grasp objects.

Experiment

To recognize the important role joints play

Imagine that you have no knees—just one long bone in each leg. Go for a walk around your home. If there are stairs, try to climb them. What did you discover? Try this experiment imagining you had no elbows. What things can't you do?

Explanation: If our skeleton was made of only one bone, we'd be stiff as a board. Our joints help us move in all kinds of wonderful ways.

Amazing Facts!

✔ Fixed joints are designed to barely move at all. One place you find fixed joints is in your skull.

✔ When you take a spoonful of soup, more than thirty joints move in your fingers, wrist, arm, and shoulder. Many of these are sliding joints in your wrist.

Healthy Advice

✔ Cracking your knuckles can be a very annoying habit, especially to those around you. The sound really bothers many people, like parents and teachers. And habits of any kind are hard to break.

Muscles

It's a fact that's quite well known—
Your bones cannot move on their own.
If they could, then you might see
A skeleton climb up a tree.
But that can never, ever be!
For muscles are what help you climb.
Why, you use muscles ALL the time!

When you—
Kick your feet,
Walk down the street,
Or fan yourself
In the summer's heat,
Eat a beet,
Fold a sheet,
Or shake hands
With someone you meet.
With muscles, nothing can compete!

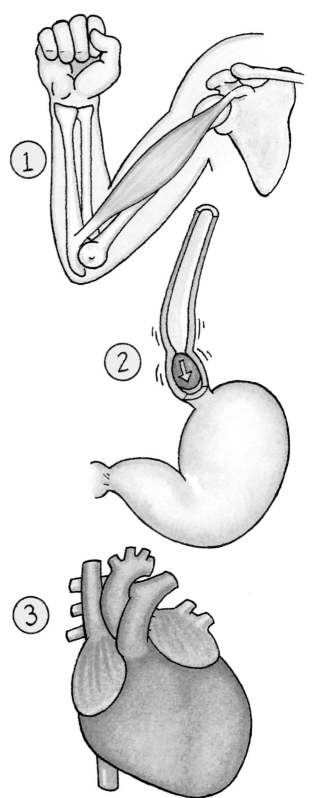

There are three different kinds of muscles:

1 *Skeletal muscles* that move your bones.

2 *Involuntary muscles* that you don't think about controlling. Examples are the muscles that move the food along once you've swallowed it.

3 The *cardiac muscle,* or heart.

Experiment

To learn about the muscles in your face

Look in a mirror and time yourself for a minute. How many different emotions can your face express?

Explanation: Sixteen different muscles in your face work together to produce hundreds of different expressions.

Amazing Facts!

✔ You have more than 600 muscles. They make up almost half of your weight!

✔ Muscles come in all different shapes—flat, round, long, thin, and even diamond shaped.

✔ Your tongue is a muscle.

✔ You use your muscles even when you're sleeping. Sometimes people change positions thirty to forty times a night.

Experiment

To feel your muscles at work

Stretch one arm straight out in front of you, palm up. With your other hand grip the muscle in the front of your upper arm (your *biceps*). Bend your arm. What do you feel happening to the biceps muscle?

Explanation: When muscles move bones, they do it by contracting. That means they "bunch up," getting shorter and fatter. When you bend your arm, you're actually feeling your biceps muscle contracting.

Healthy Advice

✔ Your muscles need to be flexible, so it's very important to stretch every day, especially before you start playing hard.

✔ Your muscles need exercise to get bigger and stronger. Running helps build leg strength, and climbing trees helps build up arm muscles.

Mouth

Your mouth is like a house,
The teeth and tongue live inside.
At the front door are your lips,
Which can close or open wide.
Just think how many visitors
You welcome here each year.
You greet them,
Then you eat them,
Chomp, chomp, chomp—they disappear!

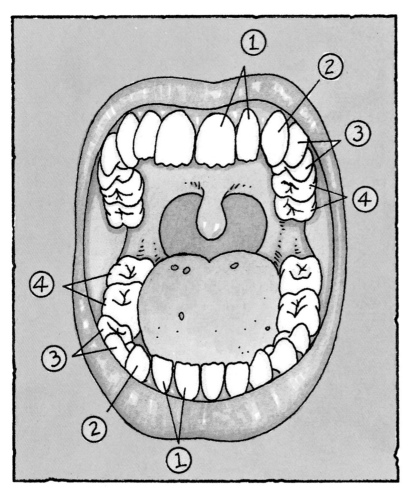

Your teeth in front
Are incisors and canines.
Next come bicuspids,
And the molars are behind.
Front teeth cut and tear,
Back teeth grind and chew.
And all together,
When you're grown,
You'll have thirty-two.

1 Incisors

2 Canines

3 Bicuspids

4 Molars

Experiment

To show how your lips and tongue help you communicate

Wash your hands, open your mouth, and hold on to your tongue so it won't move. Say "two terrific toys." What happened? Next hold your lips open so they can't touch and say "Peter picked pickles." What happened?

Explanation: You need help from your lips and tongue in order to make certain sounds clearly. When lips and tongue can't move, words get distorted.

Healthy Advice

✔ When food is left behind in your mouth after eating, germs feed on it and produce an acid that causes your teeth to decay. You need remove it by brushing and flossing every day. Since most of the food gets caught between your teeth where a toothbrush can't reach, flossing becomes especially important.

Experiment

To understand why it helps to chew your food

Find two cubes of sugar. Crush one and leave the other whole. Drop them each into a separate glass of water and stir. Which dissolves in the water faster?

Explanation: Before the food you eat can be used by your body, it has to dissolve into your blood. Foods that are ground up dissolve faster. Your stomach does most of this job, but you can help your stomach out by chewing your food well.

Amazing Facts!

✔ You actually get two full sets of teeth—twenty baby teeth when you and your mouth are little, and 32 when you and your mouth get bigger.

✔ The hardest substance in your body is the enamel covering on your teeth. It's even harder than bone!

43

Digestion

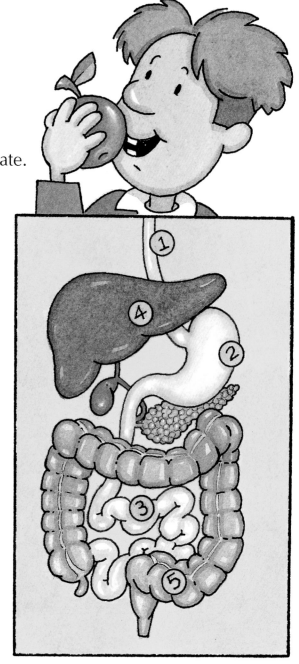

At the end of a meal
Your body must deal
With the feast that was once on your plate.
The food's broken down,
Then it's carried around
By your blood at a nice steady rate.
It reaches each part
So that each part can start
To get power from what you just ate.

1 After you swallow the food, tiny muscles push it down the *esophagus,* or the tube between your throat and your stomach.

2 The food is moved along into your stomach, where it gets churned up by stomach muscles and mixed with juices that break it down even more.

3 When food leaves your stomach, it looks like a thick liquid. Next it is pushed into your small intestine.

4 Digestive juices from your liver and pancreas are poured over the food in your small intestine. When digestion is complete, nutrients are absorbed, and blood carries them throughout your body.

5 The parts of food that your body can't use move into the large intestine. Then they get passed out of your body when you make a bowel movement.

Experiment

To understand the importance of saliva

Take a small piece of bread and place it on your tongue. Close your mouth and hold it there for about a minute. What happens?

Explanation: Saliva is a special juice that starts digestion by breaking down food even before you swallow.

Healthy Advice

✔ Be sure to chew your food well and not rush through meals.

✔ Be sure not to eat too many candies or sweets. They fill you up, but don't give your body much of what it needs to stay healthy

✔ Remember that no single food can give your body everything it needs to stay healthy. Every day you need to eat a wide variety of foods, including fruits and vegetables, dairy products, meat and meat alternates, and cereals and breads.

Experiment

To understand how swallowing works

With the help of a friend, and using a soft pillow, stand on your head. Now drink a sip of water through a straw. Can you swallow?

Explanation: Food and drink don't just fall into your stomach. It is pushed along by tiny muscles line your *esophagus,* or the tube between your throat and your stomach.

Amazing Facts!

✔ You can listen to digestion at work! About a half hour after eating, put your ear to a friend's stomach and listen to the rumbling, sloshing, and gurgling.

✔ Your small intestines are between twenty and thirty feet long. That's four or five times as tall as you are!

✔ Food can take as long as twelve hours to make the trip all the way through your digestive system.

The Whole Works

All parts of you
Have jobs to do
In the human body symphony.
Together they
Join into play,
All parts in perfect harmony.

Your heart pumps the blood with
    perfection,
Creating a strong rhythm section.
Piping the air in and out
Is what respiration's about.
The digestive system, you see,
Gives the symphony its energy.

The muscular tones,
Supported by bones,
Give structure and flow
Wherever you go.
And it's perfectly plain
That your fabulous brain
These parts large and small
Conducts one and all.

Step right up and shout it loud—
My body's great and I am proud!
There's no one else I'd rather be.
I treasure the pleasure of being me!

Other children's books from Fairview Press

Alligator in the Basement, by Bob Keeshan, TV's Captain Kangaroo
illustrated by Kyle Corkum

Box-Head Boy, by Christine M. Winn with David Walsh, Ph.D.
illustrated by Christine M. Winn

Clover's Secret, by Christine M. Winn with David Walsh, Ph.D.
illustrated by Christine M. Winn

Hurry, Murray, Hurry!, by Bob Keeshan, TV's Captain Kangaroo
illustrated by Glenn Quist

Monster Boy, by Christine M. Winn with David Walsh, Ph.D.
illustrated by Christine M. Winn

My Dad Has HIV, by Earl Alexander, Sheila Rudin, Pam Sejkora
illustrated by Ronnie Walter Shipman

"Wonderful You" Series, by Slim Goodbody
illustrated by Terry Boles
The Body
The Mind
The Spirit